D0888405

Stay Positive

Hope is believing that miracles are possible!

Marci

Blue Mountain Arts®
Boulder, Colorado

Monday, December 26, 2016

First Day of Kwanzaa (USA)
Boxing Day (Canada/UK/Australia)
St. Stephen's Day (Ireland)

Tuesday, December 27, 2016

Bank Holiday (UK)

Wednesday, December 28, 2016

Thursday, December 29, 2016

Friday, December 30, 2016

Saturday, December 31, 2016

Sunday, January 1, 2017

New Year's Day

Stay Positive

Oftentimes our path seems to be filled with roadblocks, and we wonder why life is so difficult. Things happen that leave us feeling as though we have little control over our circumstances. This is a time to remember that hope is a gift we can give to ourselves... When we choose this attitude and tap into our inner reserves, we are rewarded with the knowledge of what we have learned in life. The decision to look forward, stay positive, and remain hopeful is a key that unlocks the door to possibilities, and, when shared, returns to renew the spirit. May hope be your blessing every day.

Hope is believing that miracles are possible!

January 2017

Sunday	Monday	Tuesday	Wednesday
1 New Year's Day	2 Bank Holiday (UK)	3 Bank Holiday (Scotland)	4
8	9	10	11
15	16 Martin Luther King, Jr.'s Birthday Observed (USA)	17	18
22	23	24	25
29	30	31	

Thursday	Friday	Saturday	Notes
5	6	7	
	Epiphany		
12	13	14	
Full Moon ○			
19	20	21	
26	27	28	
Australia Day (Australia)		Chinese New Year	

December 2016

S	M	T	W	T	F	S
				1	2	3
4	5	6	7	8	9	10
11	12	13	14	15	16	17
18	19	20	21	22	23	24
25	26	27	28	29	30	31

February

S	M	T	W	T	F	S
			1	2	3	4
5	6	7	8	9	10	11
12	13	14	15	16	17	18
19	20	21	22	23	24	25
26	27	28				

Monday, January 2

Bank Holiday (UK)

Tuesday, January 3

Bank Holiday (Scotland)

Wednesday, January 4

Thursday, January 5

Friday, January 6

Saturday, January 7

Sunday, January 8

There are two days in the week that are not important... yesterday and tomorrow. Focus on today.

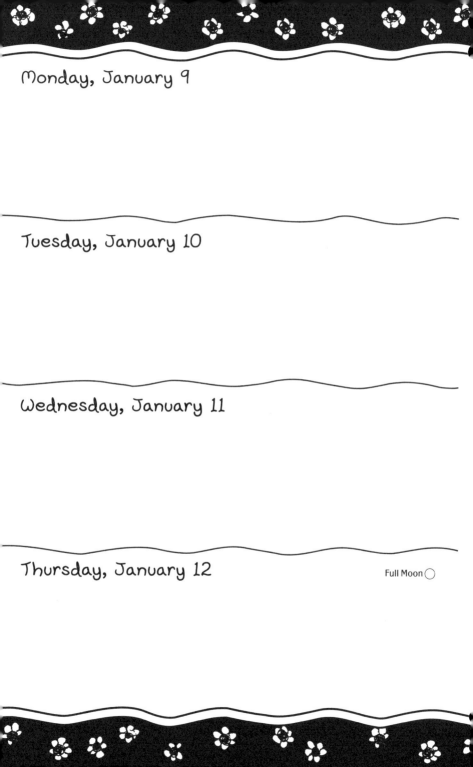

Monday, January 9

Tuesday, January 10

Wednesday, January 11

Thursday, January 12

Full Moon ○

Friday, January 13

Saturday, January 14

Sunday, January 15

Remember that dreams are the start
of every great adventure. When you
close your eyes and imagine your happy
and successful self in the future, you
are beginning your journey!

Monday, January 16

Hope

Tuesday, January 17

Wednesday, January 18

Thursday, January 19

Friday, January 20

Saturday, January 21

Sunday, January 22

Remember that by your actions you can uplift the spirit of another, and when you are both having a rough day, this is the fastest route to happiness!

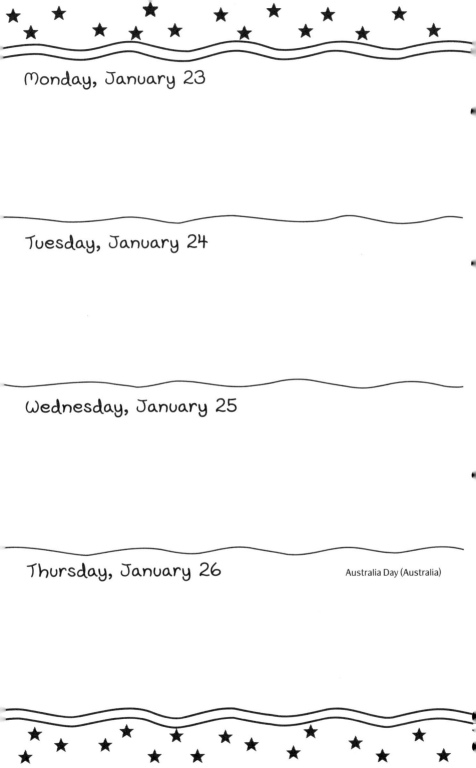

Monday, January 23

Tuesday, January 24

Wednesday, January 25

Thursday, January 26   Australia Day (Australia)

Friday, January 27

Saturday, January 28

Chinese New Year

Sunday, January 29

We each have a chance every day to brighten the life of another. It can be a kind smile... a simple hello... shared inspiration... or an unexpected gesture to let someone know that their being in the world makes a difference.

Monday, January 30

Tuesday, January 31

Wednesday, February 1 Black History Month Begins

Thursday, February 2 Groundhog Day

Friday, February 3

Saturday, February 4

Sunday, February 5

Write down your dreams
and tuck them away,
entrusting that all things
will come at the right time.

February 2017

Sunday	Monday	Tuesday	Wednesday
May hope be a constant in your life... a gift to yourself and others.			1 — Black History Month Begins
5	6 — Waitangi Day (New Zealand)	7	8
12 — Lincoln's Birthday (USA)	13	14 — Valentine's Day	15
19	20 — Presidents' Day (USA)	21	22 — Washington's Birthday (USA)
26	27	28	

Thursday	Friday	Saturday	Notes
2 Groundhog Day	3	4	
9	10 Full Moon ○	11	
16	17	18	
23	24	25	

January

S	M	T	W	T	F	S
1	2	3	4	5	6	7
8	9	10	11	12	13	14
15	16	17	18	19	20	21
22	23	24	25	26	27	28
29	30	31				

March

S	M	T	W	T	F	S
			1	2	3	4
5	6	7	8	9	10	11
12	13	14	15	16	17	18
19	20	21	22	23	24	25
26	27	28	29	30	31	

Monday, February 6

Waitangi Day (New Zealand)

Tuesday, February 7

Wednesday, February 8

Thursday, February 9

Friday, February 10

Full Moon ○

Saturday, February 11

Sunday, February 12

Lincoln's Birthday (USA)

Here's a
Hug of
Encouragement

When you need encouragement, remember these things:

You are stronger than you realize.

Life's inevitable adversities call forth our courage.

You have a lot of wisdom inside you.

God's plan will unfold with perfect timing.

The voice of your soul will lead the way.

Monday, February 13

Tuesday, February 14

Wednesday, February 15

Thursday, February 16

Friday, February 17

Saturday, February 18

Sunday, February 19

Remember that you are special.
There are talents locked away
inside you just waiting for the
right time to unfold.

Monday, February 20

Presidents' Day (USA)

Tuesday, February 21

Wednesday, February 22

Washington's Birthday (USA)

Thursday, February 23

Friday, February 24

Saturday, February 25

Sunday, February 26

You are goodness and light,
and when you share that
part of yourself, you will
discover pure joy.

Monday, February 27

Tuesday, February 28

Wednesday, March 1
Ash Wednesday
St. David's Day (Wales)

Thursday, March 2

Friday, March 3

Saturday, March 4

Sunday, March 5

Be compassionate...
life is difficult, and
people are often working
through private battles.

March 2017

Sunday	Monday	Tuesday	Wednesday

February

S	M	T	W	T	F	S
			1	2	3	4
5	6	7	8	9	10	11
12	13	14	15	16	17	18
19	20	21	22	23	24	25
26	27	28				

April

S	M	T	W	T	F	S
						1
2	3	4	5	6	7	8
9	10	11	12	13	14	15
16	17	18	19	20	21	22
23/30	24	25	26	27	28	29

1
Ash Wednesday
St. David's Day (Wales)

5

6

7

8
International Women's Day

12
Purim
USA/Canada Daylight
Saving Time Begins
Full Moon ◯

13
Commonwealth Day (UK)

14

15

19

20
Spring Begins

21

22

26
Mothering Sunday (UK)
UK/Ireland Daylight
Saving Time Begins

27

28

29

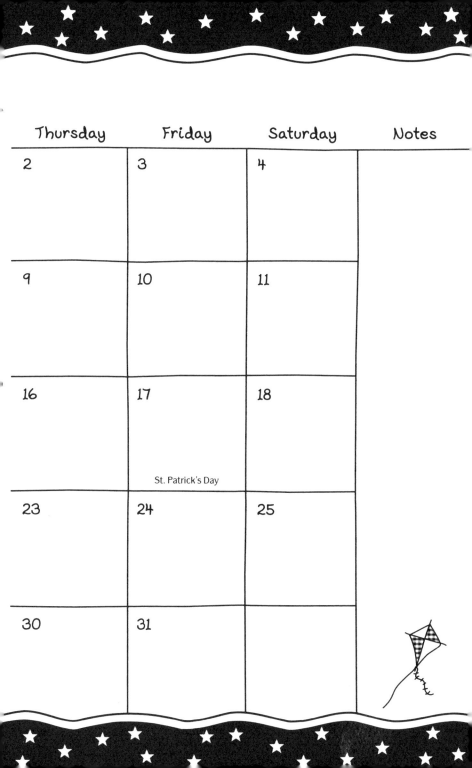

Thursday	Friday	Saturday	Notes
2	3	4	
9	10	11	
16	17 St. Patrick's Day	18	
23	24	25	
30	31		

Monday, March 6

Tuesday, March 7

Wednesday, March 8

International Women's Day

Thursday, March 9

Friday, March 10

Saturday, March 11

Sunday, March 12

Purim
USA/Canada Daylight Saving Time Begins
Full Moon ○

Everything Happens for a Reason

So often we wonder about the "whys" in life... "Why did this happen?" "Why me?" "Why now?" But there is a secret that wise men know... Bumps in the road are an inevitable part of life that soften us, make us grow, and bestow upon us the virtue of compassion. Often it is only with the passing of time that it becomes clear that the cloud really did have a silver lining and how we have wisdom, strength, and hope to share. And at last, we understand the true meaning of the phrase "Everything happens for a reason."

Monday, March 13

Commonwealth Day (UK)

Tuesday, March 14

Wednesday, March 15

Thursday, March 16

Friday, March 17

Saturday, March 18

Sunday, March 19

Your life holds for you endless possibilities.
You have built a solid foundation, and you
have worked hard for it. Continue to do
what is necessary to move
forward one day at a time.

Monday, March 20

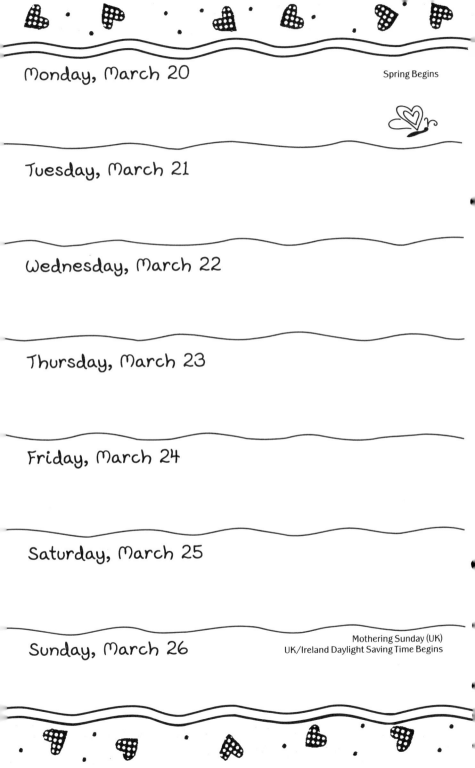

Tuesday, March 21

Wednesday, March 22

Thursday, March 23

Friday, March 24

Saturday, March 25

Sunday, March 26

Mothering Sunday (UK)
UK/Ireland Daylight Saving Time Begins

Monday, March 27

Tuesday, March 28

Wednesday, March 29

Thursday, March 30

Friday, March 31

Saturday, April 1

April Fools' Day

Sunday, April 2

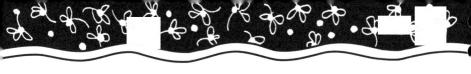

April 2017

Sunday	Monday	Tuesday	Wednesday

March

S	M	T	W	T	F	S
			1	2	3	4
5	6	7	8	9	10	11
12	13	14	15	16	17	18
19	20	21	22	23	24	25
26	27	28	29	30	31	

May

S	M	T	W	T	F	S
	1	2	3	4	5	6
7	8	9	10	11	12	13
14	15	16	17	18	19	20
21	22	23	24	25	26	27
28	29	30	31			

2	3	4	5

9	10	11	12
Palm Sunday		First Day of Passover Full Moon ◯	

16	17	18	19
Easter Sunday Orthodox Easter Sunday	Easter Monday (Canada/ UK/Ireland/Australia)		

23 St. George's Day (UK) / 30	24	25	26
	Holocaust Remembrance Day (Yom Hashoah)	Anzac Day (Australia/ New Zealand)	Administrative Professionals Day

Thursday	Friday	Saturday	Notes
You are hopes and dreams and love made visible.		1 April Fools' Day	
6	7	8	
13	14 Good Friday	15	
20	21	22 Earth Day	
27 Take Our Daughters and Sons to Work Day (USA)	28	29	

Monday, April 3

Tuesday, April 4

Wednesday, April 5

Thursday, April 6

Friday, April 7

Saturday, April 8

Sunday, April 9

Palm Sunday

Angels Are Everywhere!

Sometimes we feel that we are all alone, as life brings us challenges to overcome and hardships to bear. But when we least expect it, help can appear. It may be a kind word from a stranger or a phone call at just the right time, and we are suddenly surrounded with the loving grace of God. Miracles happen every day because angels are everywhere!

Monday, April 10

Tuesday, April 11

First Day of Passover
Full Moon ○

Wednesday, April 12

Thursday, April 13

Friday, April 14

Saturday, April 15

Sunday, April 16

Encourage someone today...
The words "everything will be
okay" can lighten the heart of
another. Share love... there
is an endless supply.

Monday, April 17

Tuesday, April 18

Wednesday, April 19

Thursday, April 20

Friday, April 21

Saturday, April 22

Earth Day

Sunday, April 23

St. George's Day (UK)

There have never been words
more powerful than "I love you"...
or more meaningful than
"Thank you"...
or more sustaining than
"I believe in you."

Monday, April 24   Holocaust Remembrance Day (Yom Hashoah)

Tuesday, April 25   Anzac Day (Australia/New Zealand)

Wednesday, April 26   Administrative Professionals Day

Thursday, April 27   Take Our Daughters and Sons to Work Day (USA)

Friday, April 28

Saturday, April 29

Sunday, April 30

Be hopeful... your
attitude will uplift the
spirit of another.

May 2017

Sunday	Monday	Tuesday	Wednesday
	1 May Day Bank Holiday (UK/Ireland)	2	3
7	8	9 National Teacher Day (USA)	10 Full Moon ◯
14 Mother's Day	15	16	17
21	22 Victoria Day (Canada)	23	24
28	29 Memorial Day Observed (USA) Bank Holiday (UK)	30	31 First Day of Shavuot

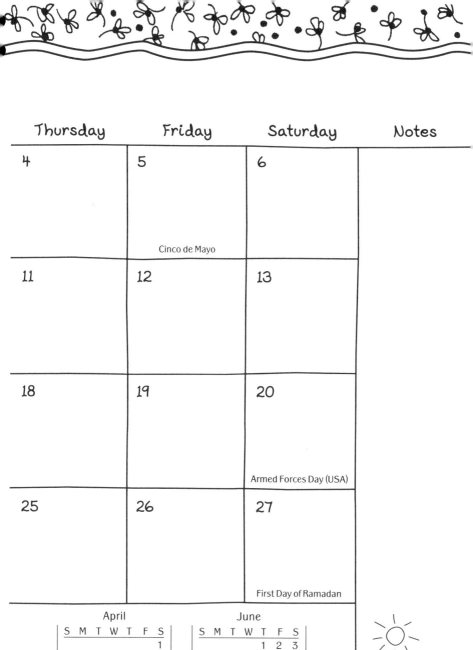

Thursday	Friday	Saturday	Notes
4	5	6	
	Cinco de Mayo		
11	12	13	
18	19	20	
		Armed Forces Day (USA)	
25	26	27	
		First Day of Ramadan	

April

S	M	T	W	T	F	S
						1
2	3	4	5	6	7	8
9	10	11	12	13	14	15
16	17	18	19	20	21	22
23/30	24	25	26	27	28	29

June

S	M	T	W	T	F	S
				1	2	3
4	5	6	7	8	9	10
11	12	13	14	15	16	17
18	19	20	21	22	23	24
25	26	27	28	29	30	

Monday, May 1

May Day
Bank Holiday (UK/Ireland)

Tuesday, May 2

Wednesday, May 3

Thursday, May 4

Friday, May 5

Cinco de Mayo

Saturday, May 6

Sunday, May 7

10 Simple Things
to Remember

1. Love is why we are here.

2. The most important day
   is today.

3. If you always do your best,
   you will not have regrets.

4. In spite of your best efforts,
   some things are out of your control.

5. Things always look better tomorrow.

6. Sometimes a wrong turn will bring you to
   exactly the right place.

7. Sometimes when you think the answer is
   "no," it's "not yet."

8. True friends share your joys, see the best in
   you, and support you through challenges.

9. God and your parents will always love you.

10. For all your accomplishments, nothing will bring
    you more happiness than the love you find.

Monday, May 8

Tuesday, May 9   National Teacher Day (USA)

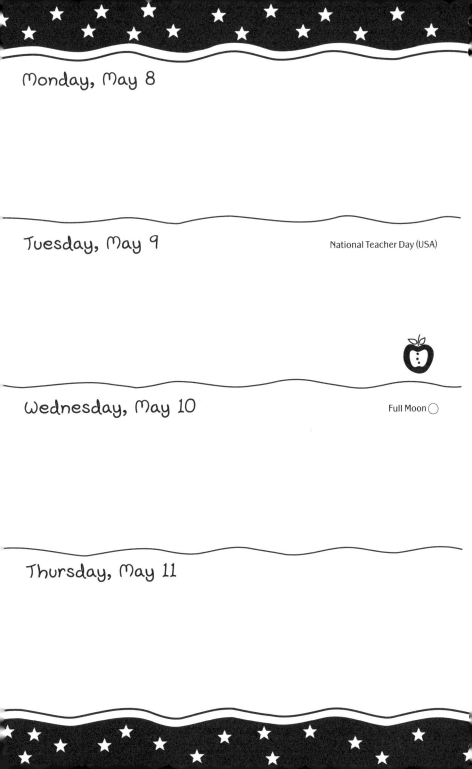

Wednesday, May 10   Full Moon ◯

Thursday, May 11

Friday, May 12

Saturday, May 13

Sunday, May 14

Mother's Day

Have Faith

Listen for that voice inside guiding you toward the right thing to do, the right path to travel, and the knowledge of what will bring you happiness and fulfillment.

Monday, May 15

Tuesday, May 16

Wednesday, May 17

Thursday, May 18

Friday, May 19

Saturday, May 20

Armed Forces Day (USA)

Sunday, May 21

If you have faith, hope, love, and the blessing of good friends, you will get through whatever challenges life brings.

Monday, May 22

Tuesday, May 23

Wednesday, May 24

Thursday, May 25

Friday, May 26

Saturday, May 27

First Day of Ramadan

Sunday, May 28

Faith is the assurance of things not seen. It is believing that a power greater than ourselves knows what is best for us and those around us.

Monday, May 29

Memorial Day Observed (USA)
Bank Holiday (UK)

Tuesday, May 30

Wednesday, May 31

First Day of Shavuot

Thursday, June 1

Friday, June 2

Saturday, June 3

Sunday, June 4

Pentecost

Cherish your friends...
remember your lives were
brought together for a reason.

June 2017

Sunday	Monday	Tuesday	Wednesday

May

S	M	T	W	T	F	S
	1	2	3	4	5	6
7	8	9	10	11	12	13
14	15	16	17	18	19	20
21	22	23	24	25	26	27
28	29	30	31			

July

S	M	T	W	T	F	S
						1
2	3	4	5	6	7	8
9	10	11	12	13	14	15
16	17	18	19	20	21	22
$^{23}/_{30}$ $^{24}/_{31}$	25	26	27	28	29	

4	5	6	7
Pentecost	Bank Holiday (Ireland)		
11	**12**	**13**	**14**
			Flag Day (USA)
18	**19**	**20**	**21**
Father's Day			Summer Begins
25	**26**	**27**	**28**
Eid al-Fitr			

Thursday	Friday	Saturday	Notes
1	2	3	
8	9	10	
	Full Moon ◯		
15	16	17	
22	23	24	
		St. Jean Baptiste Day (Québec)	
29	30		

Monday, June 5

Bank Holiday (Ireland)

Tuesday, June 6

Wednesday, June 7

Thursday, June 8

Friday, June 9

Full Moon ○

Saturday, June 10

Sunday, June 11

As You Follow Life's Path, Remember...

No matter where life takes you or what path you choose, you will always meet challenges. That is the way life is. There are no guarantees, and no matter how many things you do right or how many rules you follow, there will always be that fork in the road that makes you choose between this way or that. Whenever you meet this place, remember these things: You are loved... love will sustain you. You are strong... prayer will get you through anything. You are wise... the greatest gift of all lies within you.

FAITH
HOPE
LOVE

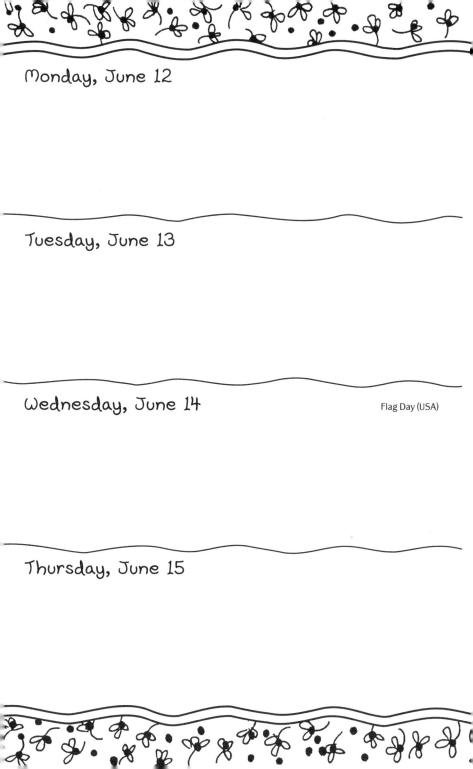

Monday, June 12

Tuesday, June 13

Wednesday, June 14   Flag Day (USA)

Thursday, June 15

Friday, June 16

Saturday, June 17

Sunday, June 18

Dad

May each day be blessed
and filled with all the
things that will bring you
lasting happiness.

Monday, June 19

Tuesday, June 20

Wednesday, June 21

Summer Begins

Thursday, June 22

Friday, June 23

Saturday, June 24

St. Jean Baptiste Day (Québec)

Sunday, June 25

Eid al-Fitr

Our Friends Are
a Blessing

Friendship is one of life's greatest treasures, and it is a gift that lasts a lifetime. We create bonds during times in our lives when our beliefs and our experiences are shaping who we are. Those bonds cannot be broken by the passing of time, even when life gets so busy that we lose touch. Let friends know that you think of them often... and they will always have a special place in your heart.

Monday, June 26

Tuesday, June 27

Wednesday, June 28

Thursday, June 29

Friday, June 30

Saturday, July 1

Canada Day (Canada)

Sunday, July 2

Give away some courage every day!
When you encourage another to
"keep going," "hang in there," or
"believe in your dreams," you will
find an unending source of happiness.

July 2017

Sunday	Monday	Tuesday	Wednesday

June

S	M	T	W	T	F	S
				1	2	3
4	5	6	7	8	9	10
11	12	13	14	15	16	17
18	19	20	21	22	23	24
25	26	27	28	29	30	

August

S	M	T	W	T	F	S
		1	2	3	4	5
6	7	8	9	10	11	12
13	14	15	16	17	18	19
20	21	22	23	24	25	26
27	28	29	30	31		

2	3	4	5
		Independence Day (USA)	
9	10	11	12
Full Moon ◯			Bank Holiday (Northern Ireland)
16	17	18	19
23 / 30	24 / 31	25	26

Thursday	Friday	Saturday	Notes
Live your beliefs... and be a powerful example of love in the world.		1 Canada Day (Canada)	
6	7	8	
13	14	15	
20	21	22	
27	28	29	

Monday, July 3

Tuesday, July 4

Independence Day (USA)

Wednesday, July 5

Thursday, July 6

Friday, July 7

Saturday, July 8

Sunday, July 9

Full Moon ◯

The Road of Life
Has Many Turns

Sometimes the road of life takes us to a place we had planned... Sometimes it shows us a surprise around the bend we could never have anticipated. We make decisions based on the information we have... We accept the ups and downs as they come... We live "one day at a time." But often we find it is only when we look back that we can see that what we had thought was a "wrong turn" has brought us to exactly the right place and every step was a right one after all!

If all else fails
get the Day

All Paths Lead
to Home

Monday, July 10

Tuesday, July 11

Wednesday, July 12   Bank Holiday (Northern Ireland)

Thursday, July 13

Friday, July 14

Saturday, July 15

Sunday, July 16

When we share "things," we divide limited resources... but when we share ourselves, we tap into the gifts within to find a renewable source of energy called love.

Monday, July 17

Tuesday, July 18

Wednesday, July 19

Thursday, July 20

Friday, July 21

Saturday, July 22

Sunday, July 23

Give to others the very
things you most need...
support, encouragement,
and hope. Giving always
goes in a circle and returns
to renew the spirit.

Monday, July 24

Tuesday, July 25

Wednesday, July 26

Thursday, July 27

Friday, July 28

Saturday, July 29

Sunday, July 30

Faith is the foundation that we come to rely on as we take our journey through life.

Monday, July 31

Tuesday, August 1

Wednesday, August 2

Thursday, August 3

Friday, August 4

Saturday, August 5

Sunday, August 6

When good things come
into your life, be inspired
to brighten the day
of another.

August 2017

Sunday	Monday	Tuesday	Wednesday
Say "thank you"... Everyone needs to be appreciated.		1	2
6	7 Civic Holiday (Canada) Bank Holiday (Ireland/Scotland) Full Moon ○	8	9
13	14	15	16
20	21	22	23
27	28 Bank Holiday (UK except Scotland)	29	30

Thursday	Friday	Saturday	Notes
3	4	5	
10	11	12	
17	18	19	
24	25	26	
31			

July

S	M	T	W	T	F	S
						1
2	3	4	5	6	7	8
9	10	11	12	13	14	15
16	17	18	19	20	21	22
23/30	24/31	25	26	27	28	29

September

S	M	T	W	T	F	S
					1	2
3	4	5	6	7	8	9
10	11	12	13	14	15	16
17	18	19	20	21	22	23
24	25	26	27	28	29	30

Monday, August 7

Civic Holiday (Canada)
Bank Holiday (Ireland/Scotland)
Full Moon ○

Tuesday, August 8

Wednesday, August 9

Thursday, August 10

Friday, August 11

Saturday, August 12

Sunday, August 13

Think of Each Day as a New Start

Sometimes we make mistakes... that is a part of our nature. We fall down because we are human and imperfect. Fortunately, each day is a chance to begin again, to wipe the slate clean, and to remember that today is the only day that exists. The past is gone... tomorrow is in the future... but today is a chance for a new start!

Monday, August 14

Tuesday, August 15

Wednesday, August 16

Thursday, August 17

Friday, August 18

Saturday, August 19

Sunday, August 20

May your steps be guided
through all of life's
challenges and your heart
remember its true calling.

Monday, August 21

Tuesday, August 22

Wednesday, August 23

Thursday, August 24

Friday, August 25

Saturday, August 26

Sunday, August 27

As you travel your journey through life, try to remember to be grateful for the things that are really important.

Monday, August 28

Bank Holiday (UK except Scotland)

Tuesday, August 29

Wednesday, August 30

Thursday, August 31

Friday, September 1

Eid al-Adha

Saturday, September 2

Sunday, September 3

We receive many gifts throughout our lives, and in time, we realize that the most precious gifts are the tiny special moments that live in our hearts and make us who we are.

September 2017

Sunday	Monday	Tuesday	Wednesday

August

S	M	T	W	T	F	S
		1	2	3	4	5
6	7	8	9	10	11	12
13	14	15	16	17	18	19
20	21	22	23	24	25	26
27	28	29	30	31		

October

S	M	T	W	T	F	S
1	2	3	4	5	6	7
8	9	10	11	12	13	14
15	16	17	18	19	20	21
22	23	24	25	26	27	28
29	30	31				

3	4	5	6
	Labor Day (USA/Canada)		Full Moon ◯
10	11	12	13
National Grandparents Day (USA)	Patriot Day (USA)		
17	18	19	20
24	25	26	27

Thursday	Friday	Saturday	Notes
	1 Eid al-Adha	2	
7	8	9	
14	15	16	
21 UN International Day of Peace Rosh Hashanah Islamic New Year	22 Autumn Begins	23	
28	29	30 Yom Kippur	

Monday, September 4   Labor Day (USA/Canada)

Tuesday, September 5

Wednesday, September 6   Full Moon ○

Thursday, September 7

Friday, September 8

Saturday, September 9

Sunday, September 10   National Grandparents Day (USA)

Choose to Be Hopeful

Hope is an attitude. It is a mental shift that we choose for ourselves as we tap into our inner reserves. When we decide to be hopeful, we open ourselves to discover the wisdom and strength we may not have known existed. When we ask ourselves to stay positive and we answer the call, we are rewarded with the knowledge of what we have learned in life. Our lessons, when viewed from this perspective, show us that things generally work out as they should. With hindsight, we are able to understand how a greater plan has been working in our lives.

Monday, September 11

Patriot Day (USA)

Tuesday, September 12

Wednesday, September 13

Thursday, September 14

Friday, September 15

Saturday, September 16

Sunday, September 17

When you share joy, it multiplies. When you share pain, it divides.

Monday, September 18

Tuesday, September 19

Wednesday, September 20

Thursday, September 21

UN International Day of Peace
Rosh Hashanah
Islamic New Year

Friday, September 22

Autumn Begins

Saturday, September 23

Sunday, September 24

May faith guide your path toward your dreams... may hope be a constant light in your life... and may love warm your heart every day.

Monday, September 25

Tuesday, September 26

Wednesday, September 27

Thursday, September 28

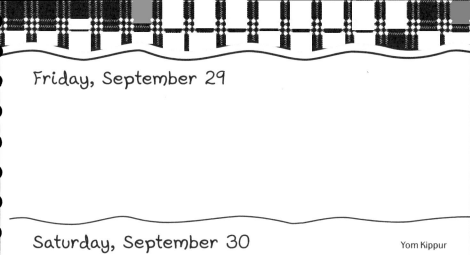

Friday, September 29

Saturday, September 30 — Yom Kippur

Sunday, October 1

Happiness is contagious.
Make someone smile, and
the good feelings come
right back to you.

October 2017

Sunday	Monday	Tuesday	Wednesday
1	2	3	4
8	9 Columbus Day Observed (USA) Thanksgiving Day (Canada)	10	11
15	16	17	18
22	23	24	25
29 UK/Ireland Daylight Saving Time Ends	30 Bank Holiday (Ireland)	31 Halloween	

Thursday	Friday	Saturday	Notes
5 First Day of Succoth Full Moon ○	6	7	
12	13	14	
19	20	21	
26	27	28	

September

S	M	T	W	T	F	S
					1	2
3	4	5	6	7	8	9
10	11	12	13	14	15	16
17	18	19	20	21	22	23
24	25	26	27	28	29	30

November

S	M	T	W	T	F	S
				1	2	3	4
5	6	7	8	9	10	11
12	13	14	15	16	17	18
19	20	21	22	23	24	25
26	27	28	29	30		

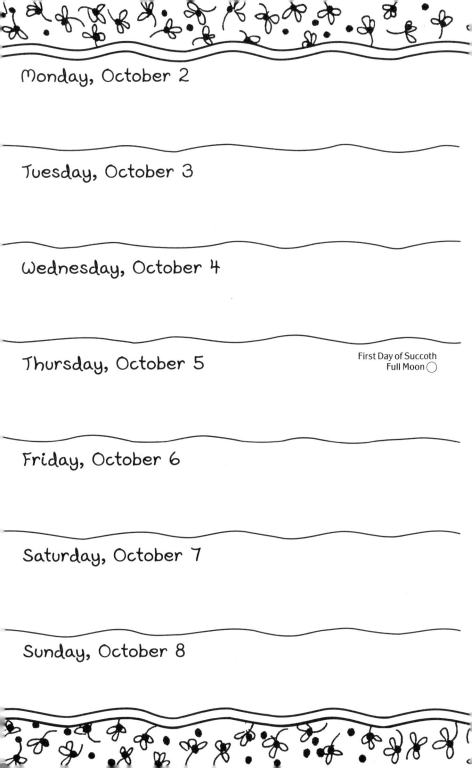

Monday, October 2

Tuesday, October 3

Wednesday, October 4

Thursday, October 5

First Day of Succoth
Full Moon ◯

Friday, October 6

Saturday, October 7

Sunday, October 8

Celebrate Life

Every day is a gift and a reason to celebrate when we remember to be grateful for the things that are really important. Life brings us joys and sorrows, struggles and triumphs, but it is our simple blessings that will get us through. Faith will light your path, hope will keep you strong, love will bring you your greatest joys, and your friendships will remind you that every day is a reason to celebrate.

Monday, October 9

Tuesday, October 10

Wednesday, October 11

Thursday, October 12

Friday, October 13

Saturday, October 14

Sunday, October 15

Handle life's ups and downs with grace and remember to encourage others along the way.

Monday, October 16

Tuesday, October 17

Wednesday, October 18

Thursday, October 19

Friday, October 20

Saturday, October 21

Sunday, October 22

May you find a place in the world that gives you a sense of contribution, the kind of love that makes the stars shine brighter, and the gift of gratitude that comes with living a life of compassion.

Monday, October 23

Tuesday, October 24

Wednesday, October 25

Thursday, October 26

Friday, October 27

Saturday, October 28

Sunday, October 29   UK/Ireland Daylight Saving Time Ends

Keep sight always of what
is important in life. Live
each day open to guidance,
and your purpose will be
revealed to you.

Monday, October 30

Bank Holiday (Ireland)

Tuesday, October 31

Halloween

Wednesday, November 1

Thursday, November 2

Friday, November 3

Saturday, November 4

Full Moon ○

Sunday, November 5

Guy Fawkes Day (UK)
USA/Canada Daylight Saving Time Ends

Your path is yours to walk;
your dreams are yours to
create; your happiness is
yours to define.

November 2017

Sunday	Monday	Tuesday	Wednesday
October / December calendars			1
5 — Guy Fawkes Day (UK) USA/Canada Daylight Saving Time Ends	6	7 — Election Day (USA)	8
12 — Remembrance Sunday (UK)	13	14	15
19	20	21	22
26	27	28	29

October

S	M	T	W	T	F	S
1	2	3	4	5	6	7
8	9	10	11	12	13	14
15	16	17	18	19	20	21
22	23	24	25	26	27	28
29	30	31				

December

S	M	T	W	T	F	S
					1	2
3	4	5	6	7	8	9
10	11	12	13	14	15	16
17	18	19	20	21	22	23
24/31	25	26	27	28	29	30

Thursday	Friday	Saturday	Notes
2	3	4 Full Moon ○	
9	10	11 Veterans Day (USA) Remembrance Day (Canada/Australia)	
16	17	18	
23 Thanksgiving Day (USA)	24	25	
30 St. Andrew's Day (Scotland)			

Monday, November 6

Tuesday, November 7

Election Day (USA)

Wednesday, November 8

Thursday, November 9

Friday, November 10

Saturday, November 11

Veterans Day (USA)
Remembrance Day (Canada/Australia)

Sunday, November 12

Remembrance Sunday (UK)

Today Is a Gift

This is a day to look forward... but also a day to look back... to see what has brought us here and to give thanks for all that has happened on the road of life. It is the love and joy we attain that warms our lives and our hearts, but it is the challenges we overcome that allow us to truly feel the glow of accomplishment. Celebrate the future... hold dear the past... and remember that "today" is the greatest gift of all!

Monday, November 13

Tuesday, November 14

Wednesday, November 15

Thursday, November 16

Friday, November 17

Saturday, November 18

Sunday, November 19

Don't Worry

Whatever is happening in your life, keep these things in mind...

Big problems can be solved in small steps.

When you are still, the gentle voice from within will guide you... listen carefully.

Remember to pray, and let God take the burden of worry from your heart.

If All Else Fails, Pet the Dog

Accept that we each learn life's lessons in our own way.

A lot of people love you more than words can say.

Monday, November 20

Tuesday, November 21

Wednesday, November 22

Thursday, November 23 Thanksgiving Day (USA)

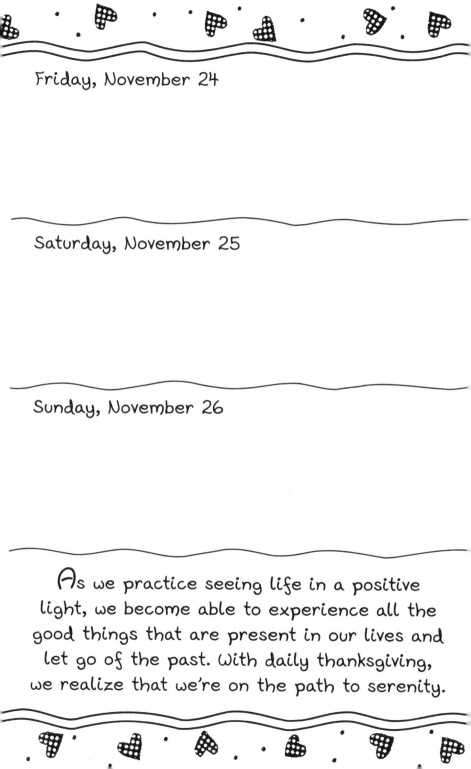

Friday, November 24

Saturday, November 25

Sunday, November 26

As we practice seeing life in a positive light, we become able to experience all the good things that are present in our lives and let go of the past. With daily thanksgiving, we realize that we're on the path to serenity.

Monday, November 27

Tuesday, November 28

Wednesday, November 29

Thursday, November 30   St. Andrew's Day (Scotland)

Friday, December 1

Saturday, December 2

Sunday, December 3

Full Moon ○

One of life's greatest gifts is gratitude, and it is free for the choosing.

Faith · Hope · Love

December 2017

Sunday	Monday	Tuesday	Wednesday

November

S	M	T	W	T	F	S
			1	2	3	4
5	6	7	8	9	10	11
12	13	14	15	16	17	18
19	20	21	22	23	24	25
26	27	28	29	30		

January 2018

S	M	T	W	T	F	S
	1	2	3	4	5	6
7	8	9	10	11	12	13
14	15	16	17	18	19	20
21	22	23	24	25	26	27
28	29	30	31			

Sunday	Monday	Tuesday	Wednesday
3 Full Moon ○	**4**	**5**	**6**
10	**11**	**12**	**13** First Day of Hanukkah
17	**18**	**19**	**20**
24 / **31**	**25** Christmas	**26** First Day of Kwanzaa (USA) Boxing Day (Canada/UK/Australia) St. Stephen's Day (Ireland)	**27**

Thursday	Friday	Saturday	Notes
	1	2	
7 National Pearl Harbor Remembrance Day (USA)	8	9	
14	15	16	
21 Winter Begins	22	23	
28	29	30	

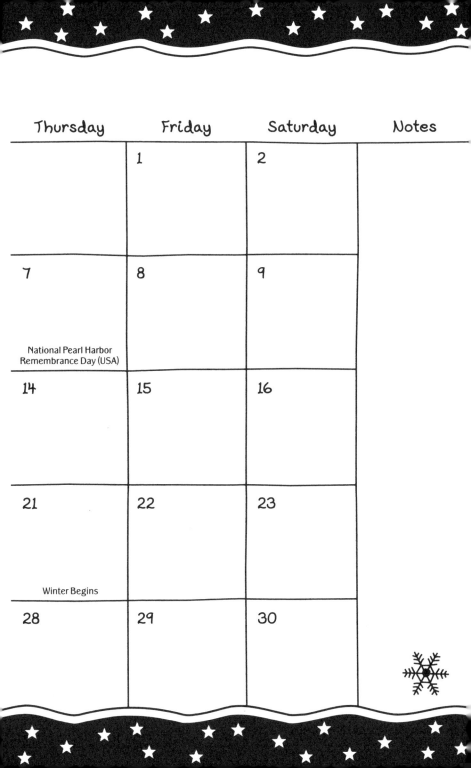

Monday, December 4

Tuesday, December 5

Wednesday, December 6

Thursday, December 7   National Pearl Harbor Remembrance Day (USA)

Friday, December 8

Saturday, December 9

Sunday, December 10

May you have a life filled with love... a true love to share your every dream... family love to warm your heart... and priceless love found in the gift of friendship.

May you find peace... peace in knowing who you are... peace in knowing what you believe in... and peace in the understanding of what is important in life.

May you find joy... joy as you awaken each day with gratitude in your heart for new beginnings... joy when you surrender to the beauty of a flower or a baby's smile... and joy, a hundred times returned, for each time you've brought happiness to another's heart.

Monday, December 11

Tuesday, December 12

Wednesday, December 13   First Day of Hanukkah

Thursday, December 14

Friday, December 15

Saturday, December 16

Sunday, December 17

May you feel the love of God like a gentle breeze when you need inspiration... may your faith remain unwavering through all of life's challenges... and may hope be the burning light that always guides your way.

Monday, December 18

Tuesday, December 19

Wednesday, December 20

Thursday, December 21

Winter Begins

Friday, December 22

Saturday, December 23

Sunday, December 24

Hold positive thoughts
in your heart and be
at peace.

Monday, December 25

Christmas

Tuesday, December 26

First Day of Kwanzaa (USA)
Boxing Day (Canada/UK/Australia)
St. Stephen's Day (Ireland)

Wednesday, December 27

Thursday, December 28

Friday, December 29

Saturday, December 30

Sunday, December 31

May hope be your blessing every day.
— Marci

Whether things are going your way or not, it's always important to remember to stay positive. This weekly planner will keep you looking on the bright side. Marci, a passionate observer of life as well as a talented artist and writer, offers a little piece of wisdom and cheerfulness every week of the year. This charming planner is illustrated with her delightful Children of the Inner Light® characters, who represent the values that are so important to us all: family, love, faith, and, above all, hope.

Blue Mountain Arts®
P.O. Box 4549, Boulder, Colorado 80306 U.S.A.

Dates for full moons and the beginnings of the seasons are in Eastern Standard Time.
Islamic holidays are calculated based on the lunar calendar and thus may vary by one or two days.

$13.95 U.S.A. $18.99 CANADA

ISBN: 978-1-68088-051-9

P9-BXR-679

CA0519

0 87400   1 6   UPC

9 781680 880519   51395   EAN